Robert Pace

TEACHING AIDS

Major Triads

U.S. $5.95

HL00372119

Distributed by HAL•LEONARD CORPORATION

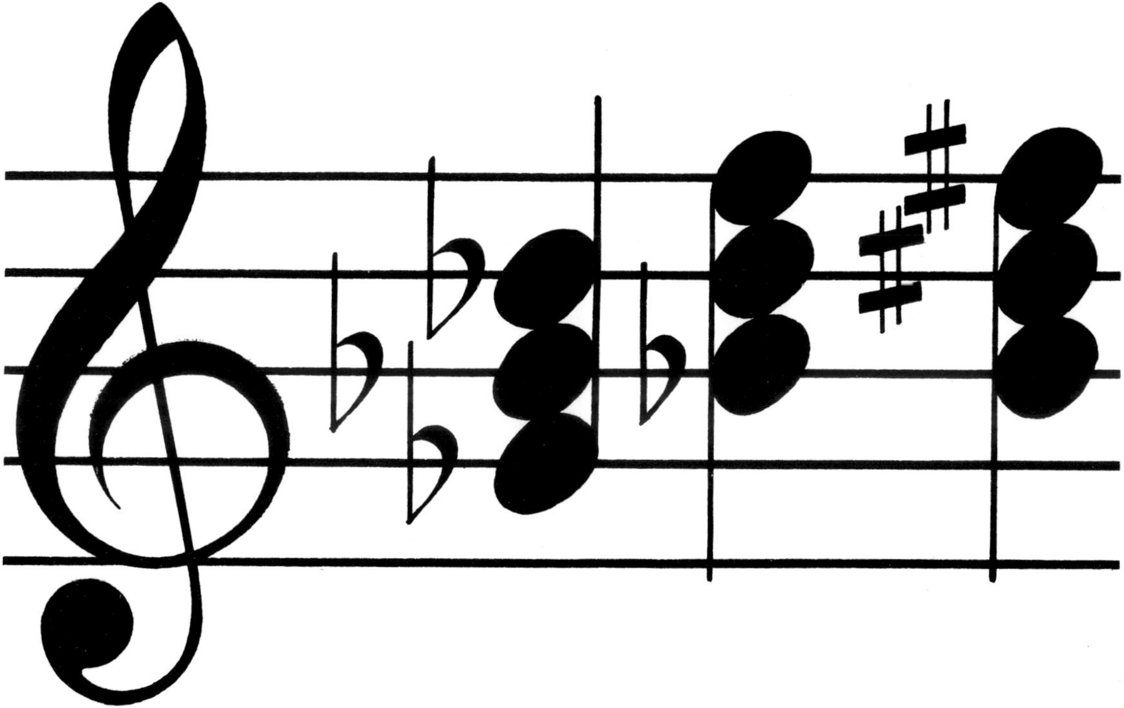

G♭ major
B♭ major
B major

LEE ROBERTS MUSIC PUBLICATIONS, INC.

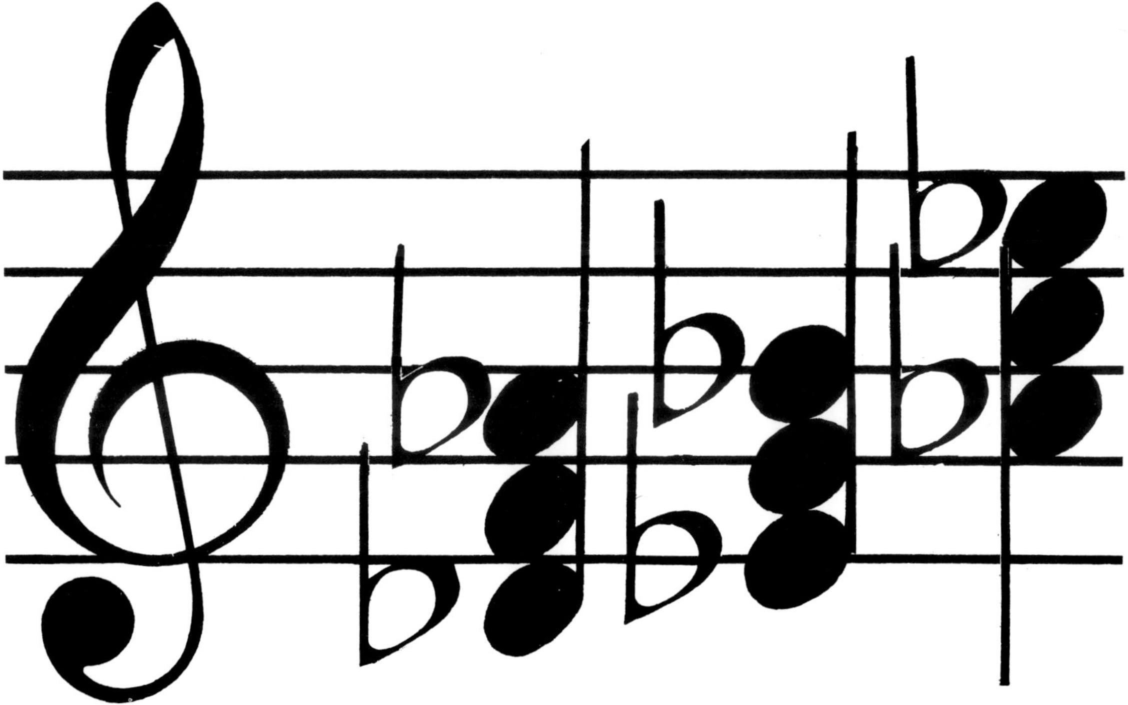

D♭ major
E♭ major
A♭ major

LEE ROBERTS MUSIC PUBLICATIONS, INC.

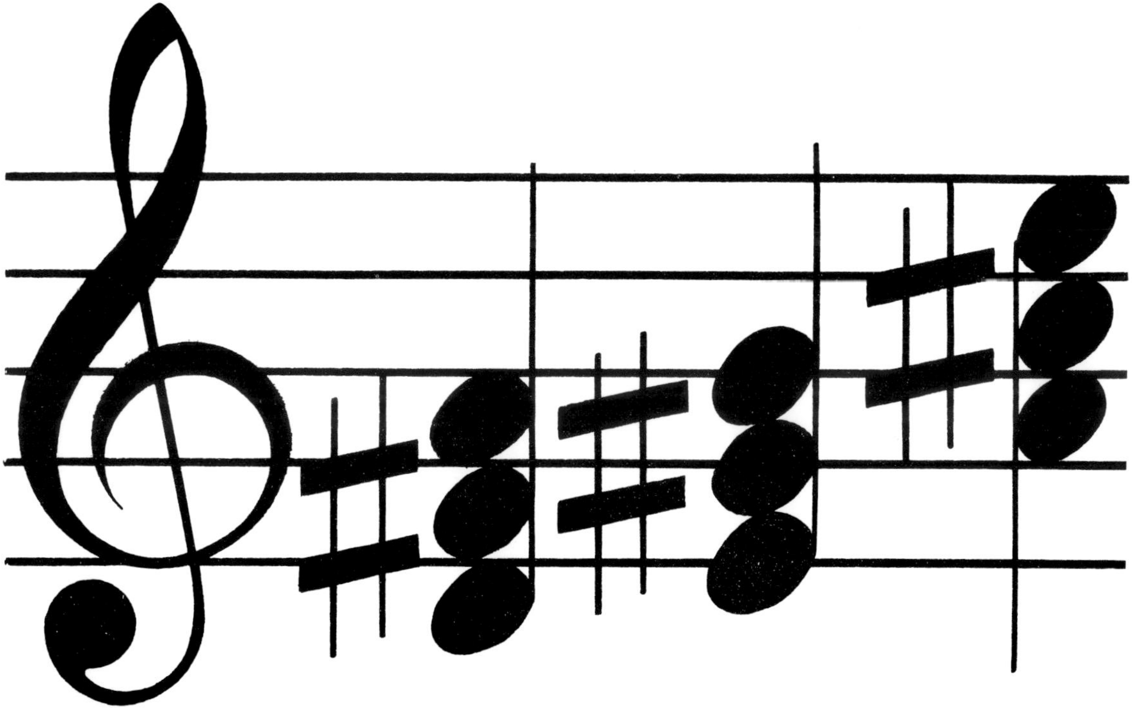

D major
E major
A major

LEE ROBERTS MUSIC PUBLICATIONS, INC.

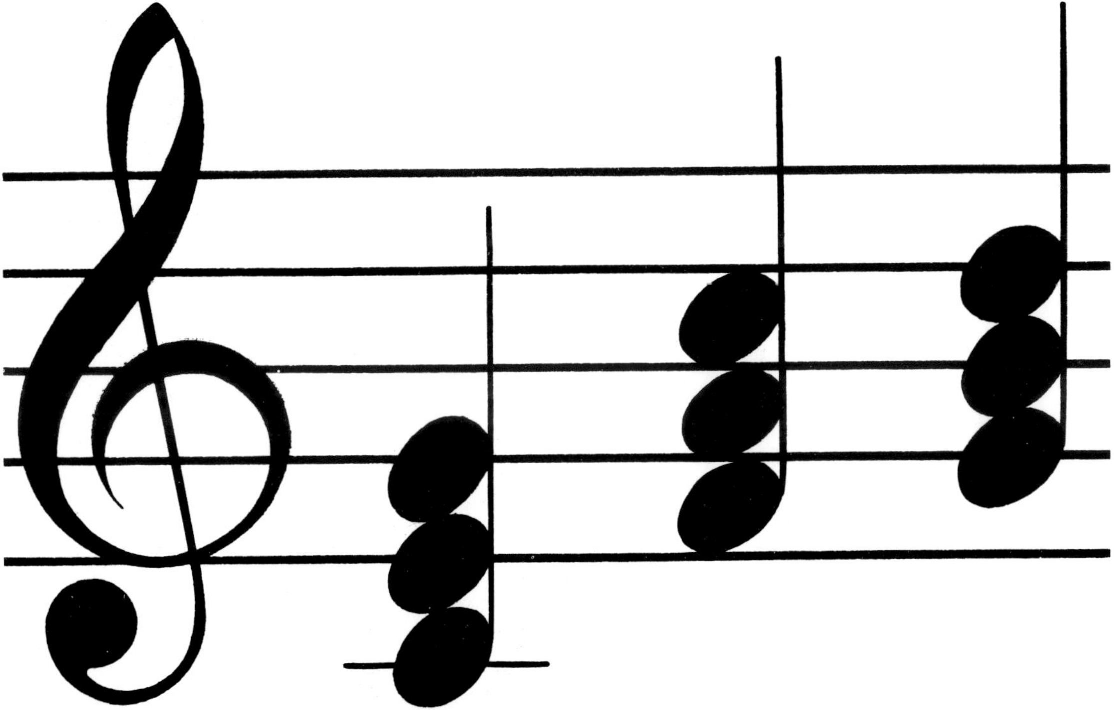

C major
F major
G major

LEE ROBERTS MUSIC PUBLICATIONS, INC.

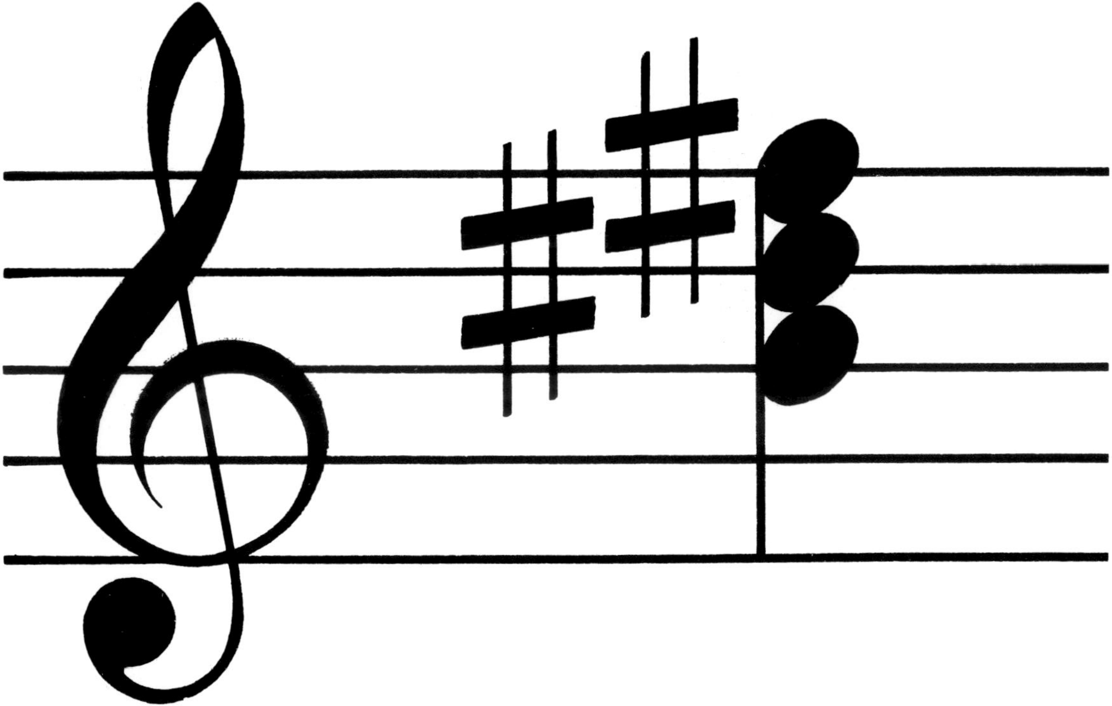

B major

LEE ROBERTS MUSIC PUBLICATIONS, INC.

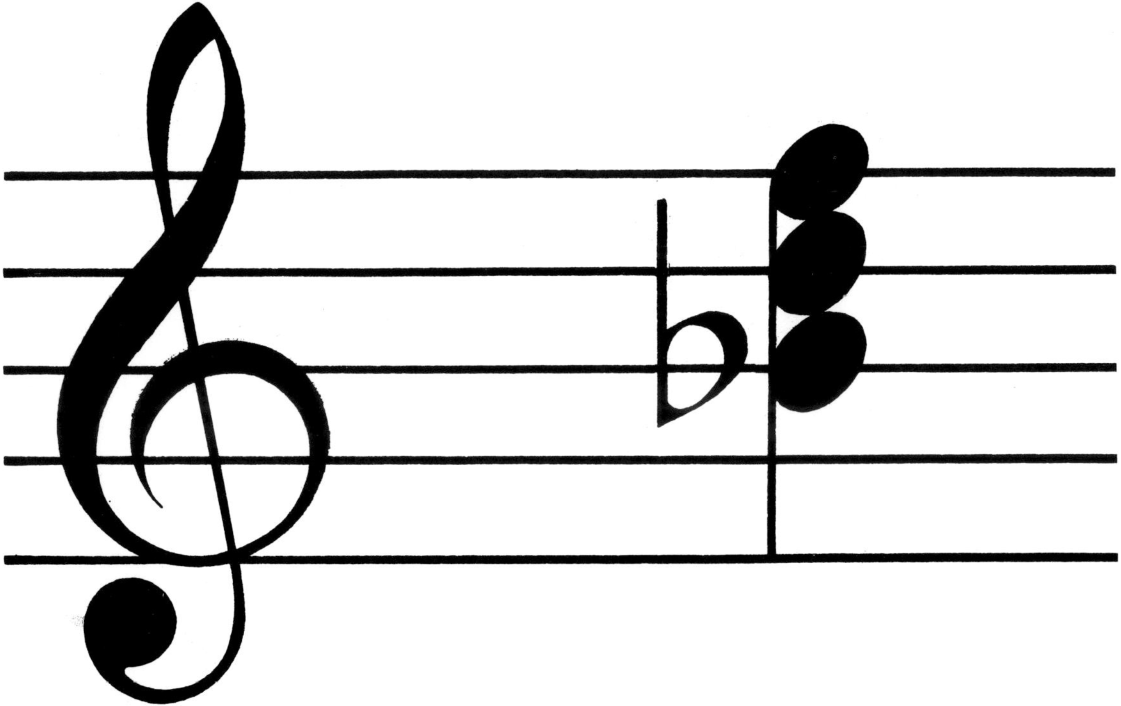

B♭ major

LEE ROBERTS MUSIC PUBLICATIONS, INC.

A major

LEE ROBERTS MUSIC PUBLICATIONS, INC.

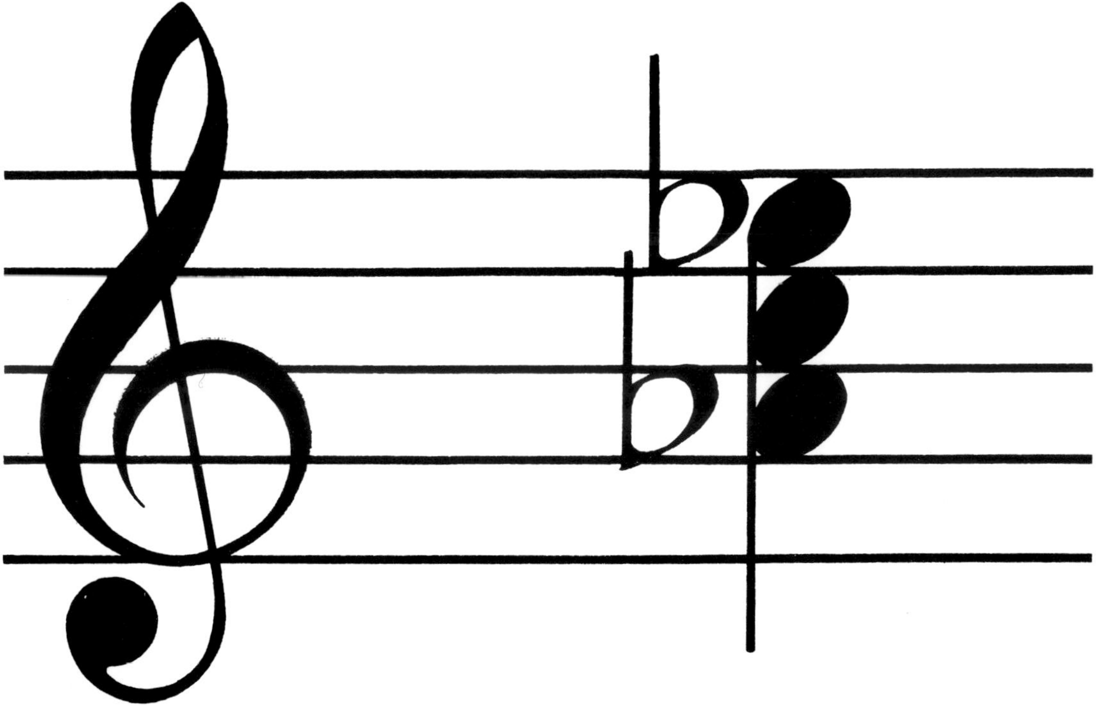

A♭ major

LEE ROBERTS MUSIC PUBLICATIONS, INC.

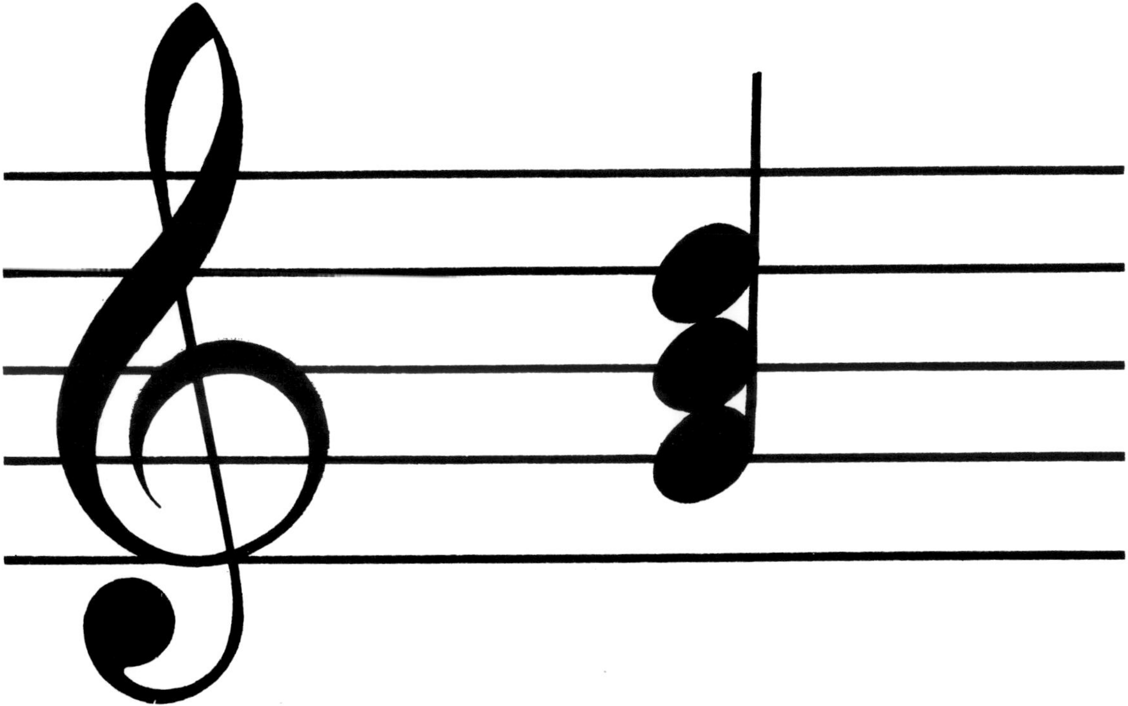

G major

LEE ROBERTS MUSIC PUBLICATIONS, INC.

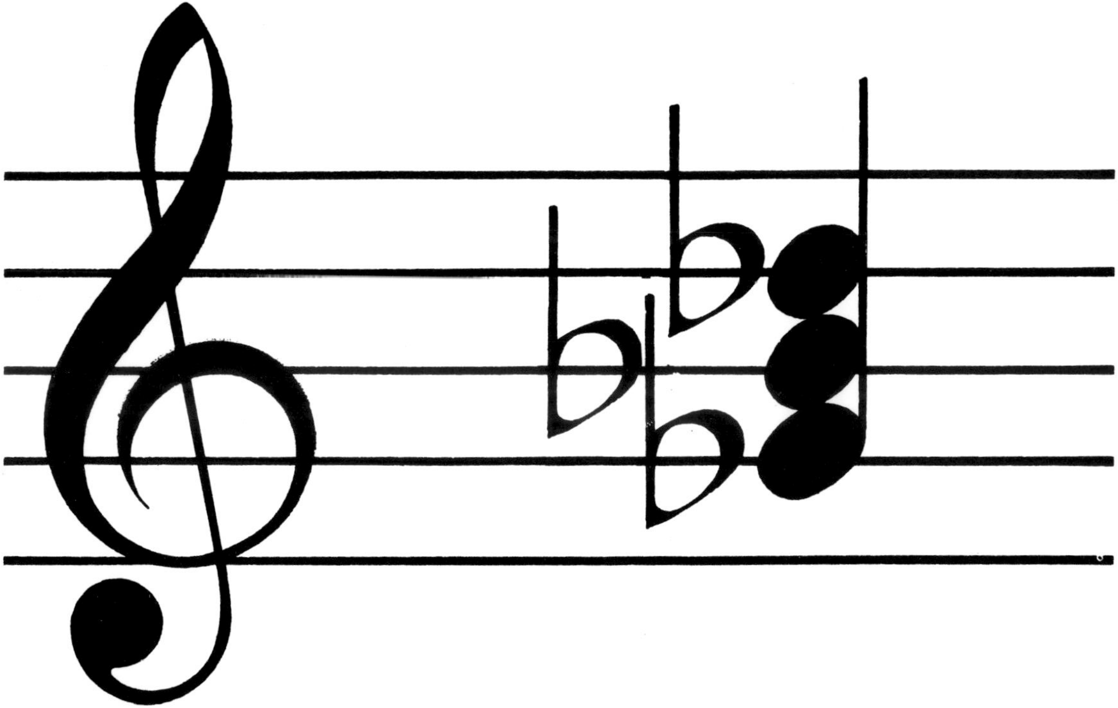

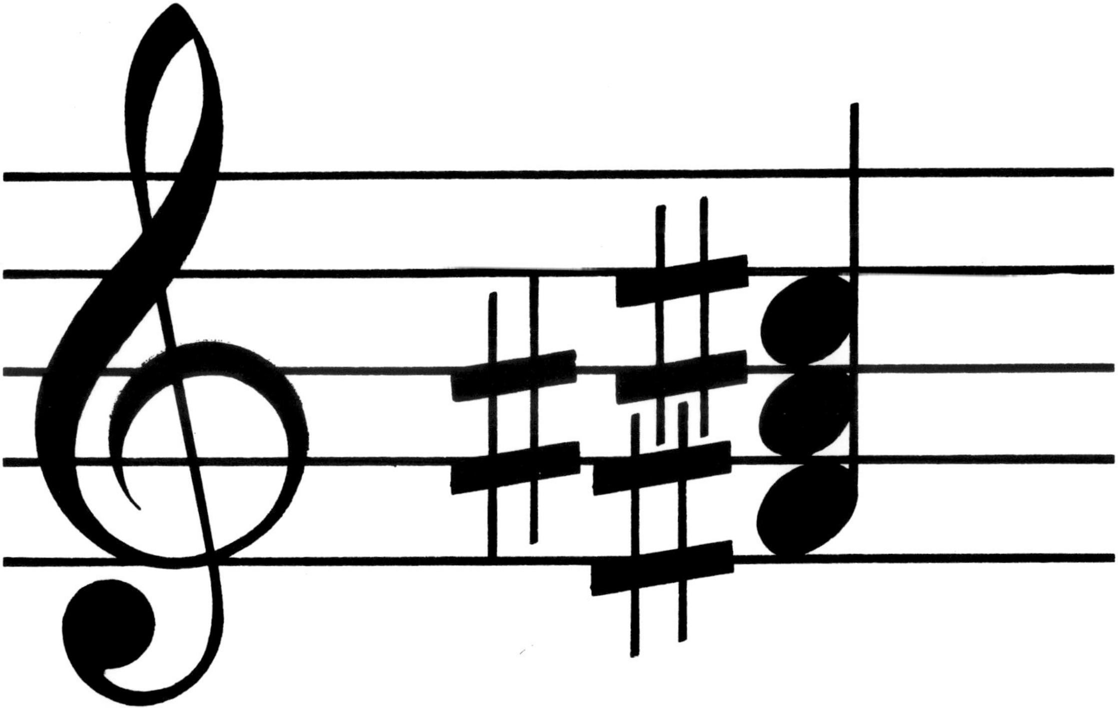

F major

LEE ROBERTS MUSIC PUBLICATIONS, INC.

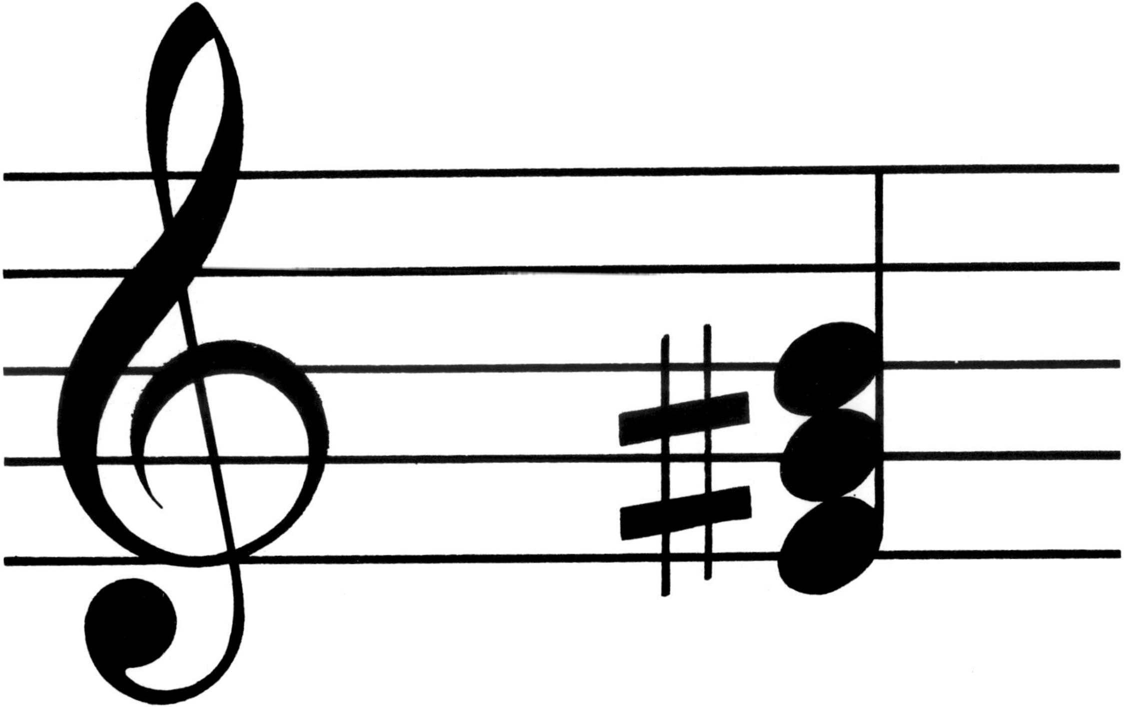

E major

LEE ROBERTS MUSIC PUBLICATIONS, INC.

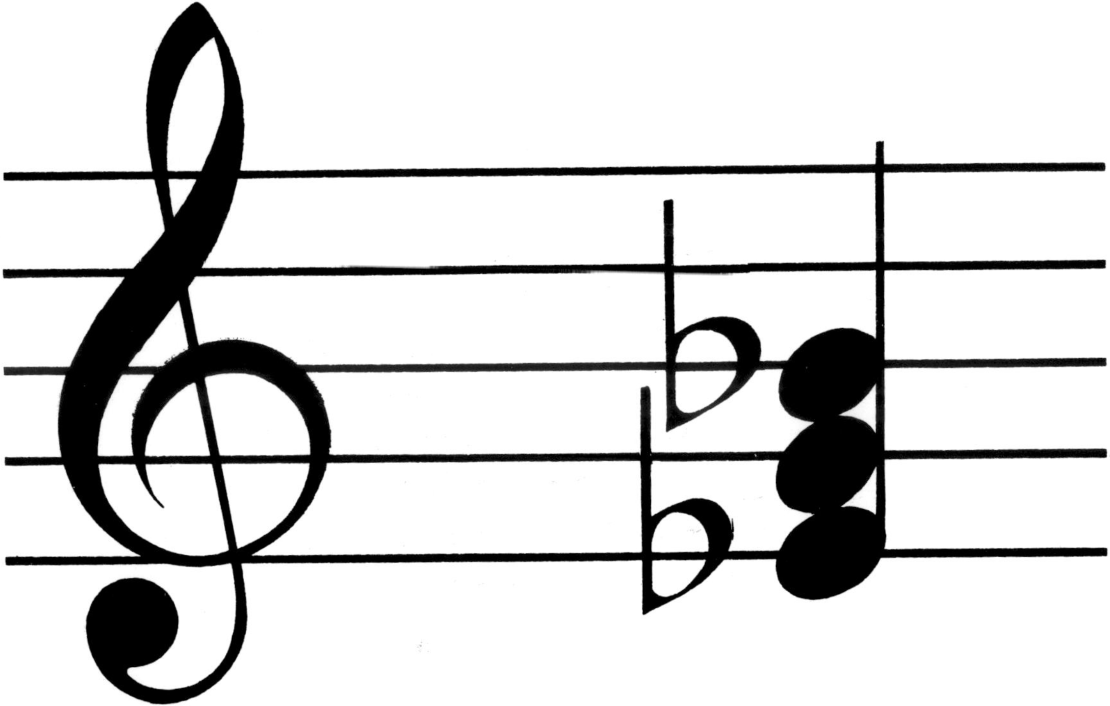

E♭ major

LEE ROBERTS MUSIC PUBLICATIONS, INC.

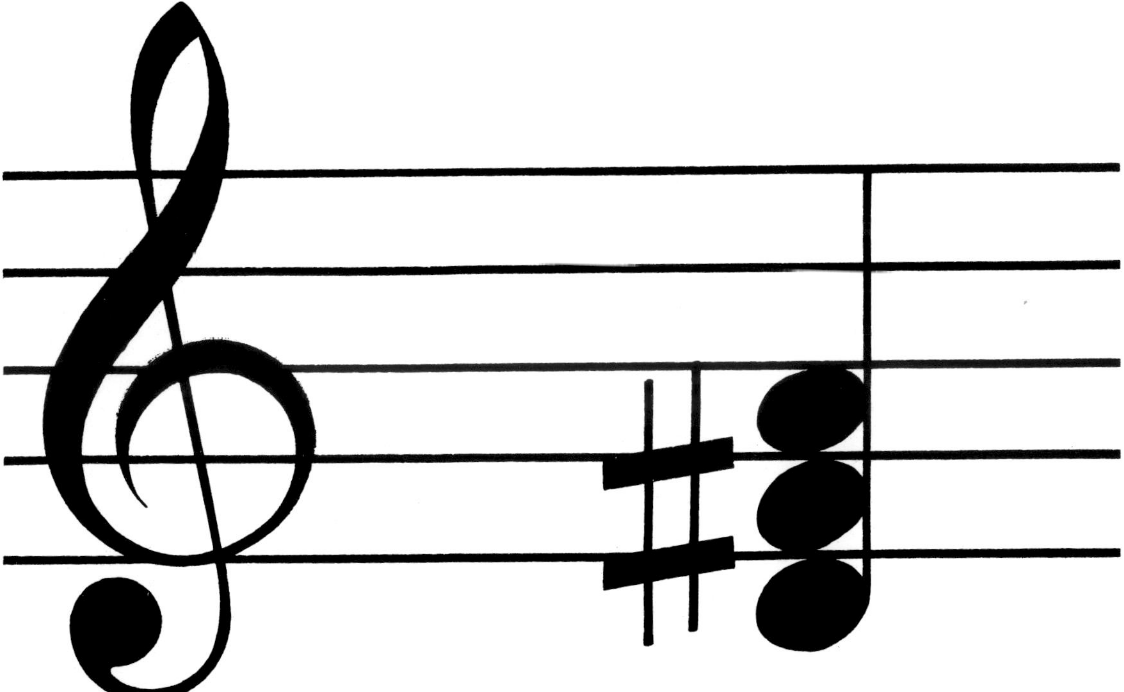

D major

LEE ROBERTS MUSIC PUBLICATIONS, INC.

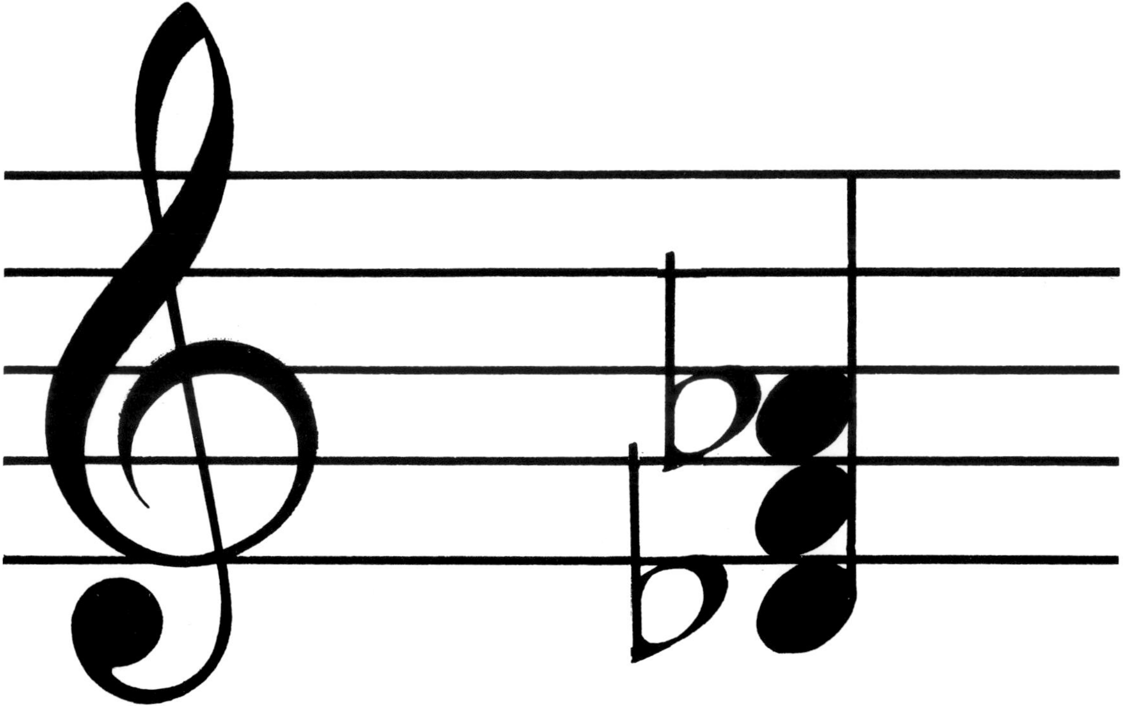

D♭ major

LEE ROBERTS MUSIC PUBLICATIONS, INC.

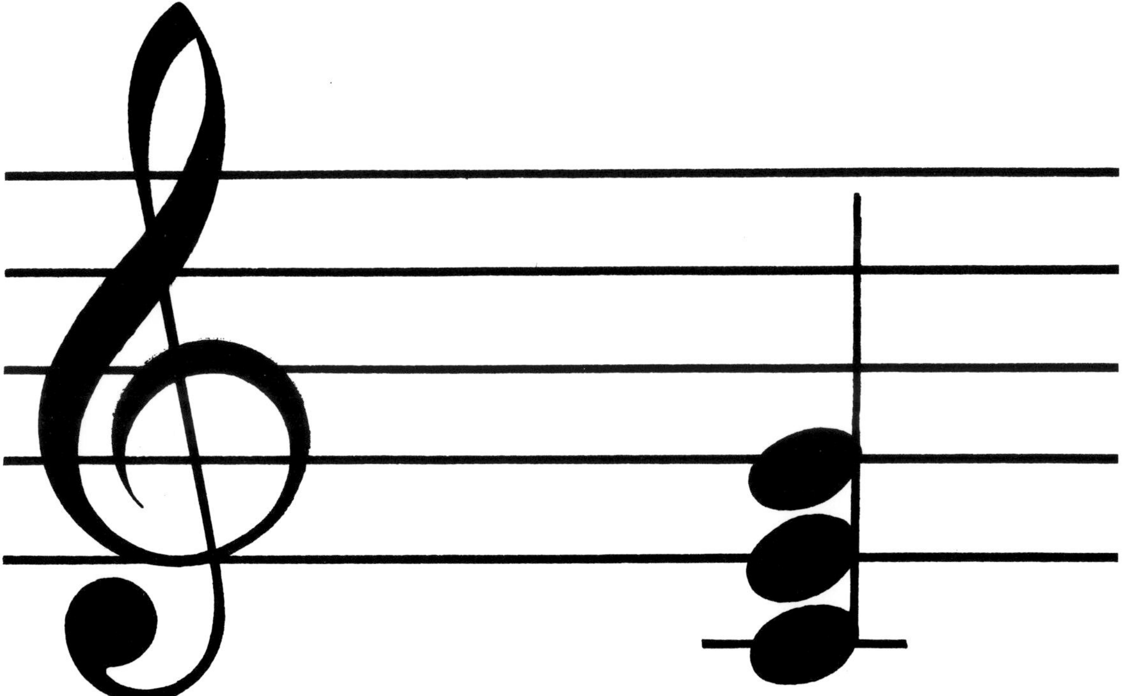

C major

LEE ROBERTS MUSIC PUBLICATIONS, INC.

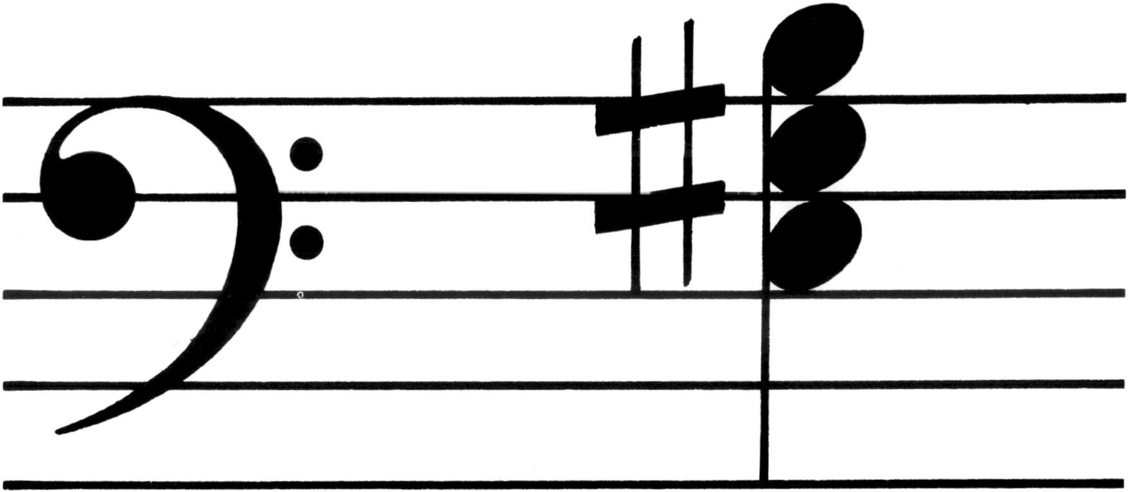

E major

LEE ROBERTS MUSIC PUBLICATIONS, INC.

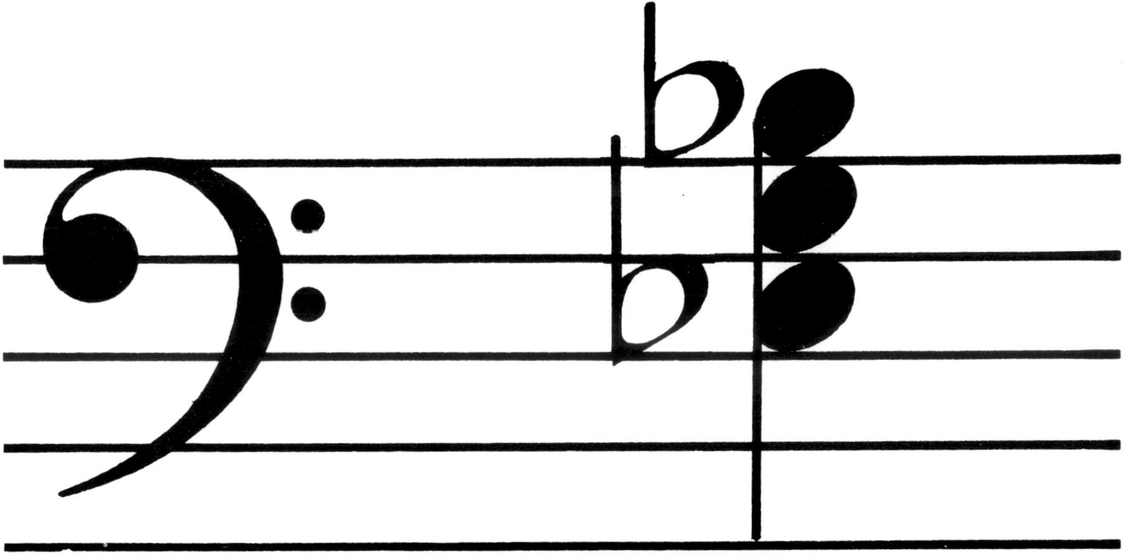

E♭ major

LEE ROBERTS MUSIC PUBLICATIONS, INC.

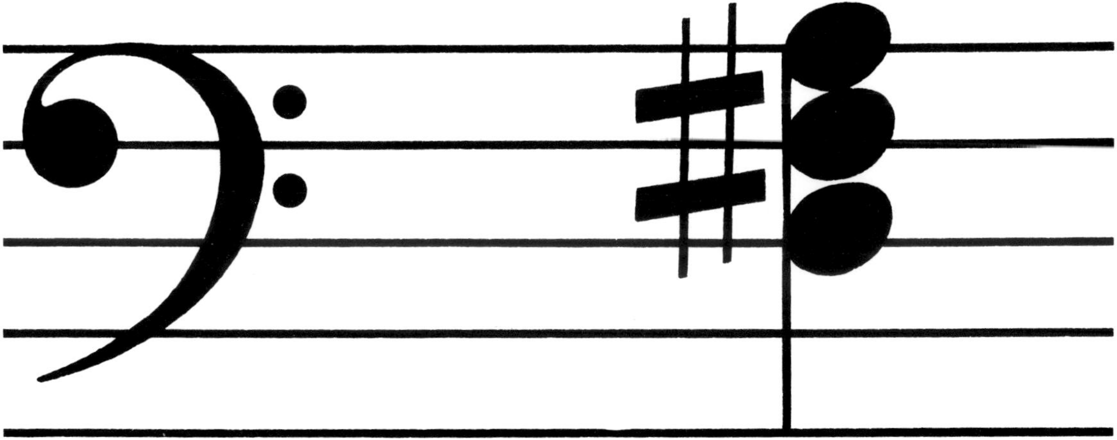

D major

LEE ROBERTS MUSIC PUBLICATIONS, INC.

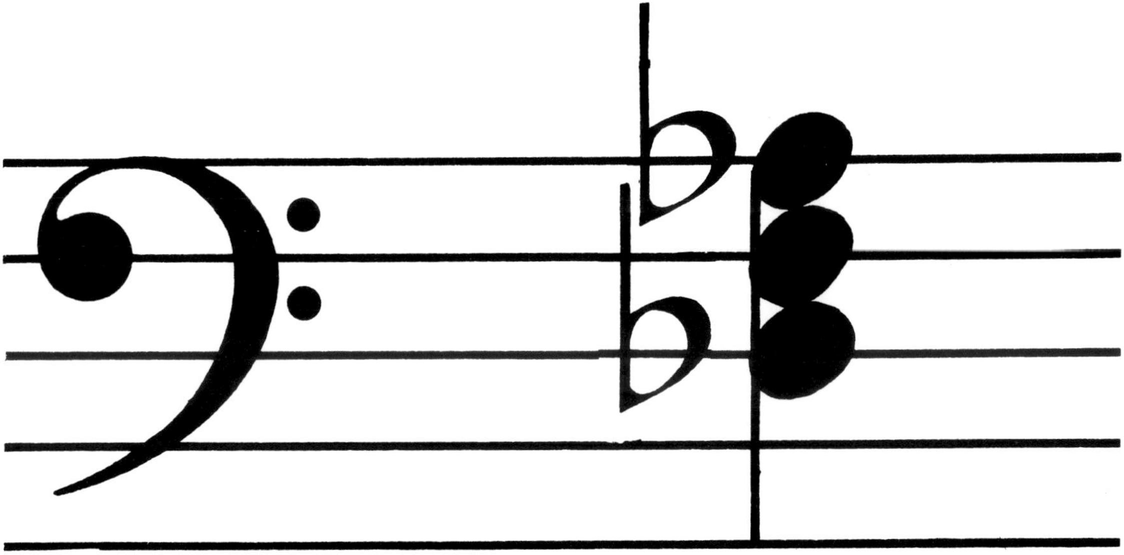

D♭ major

LEE ROBERTS MUSIC PUBLICATIONS, INC.

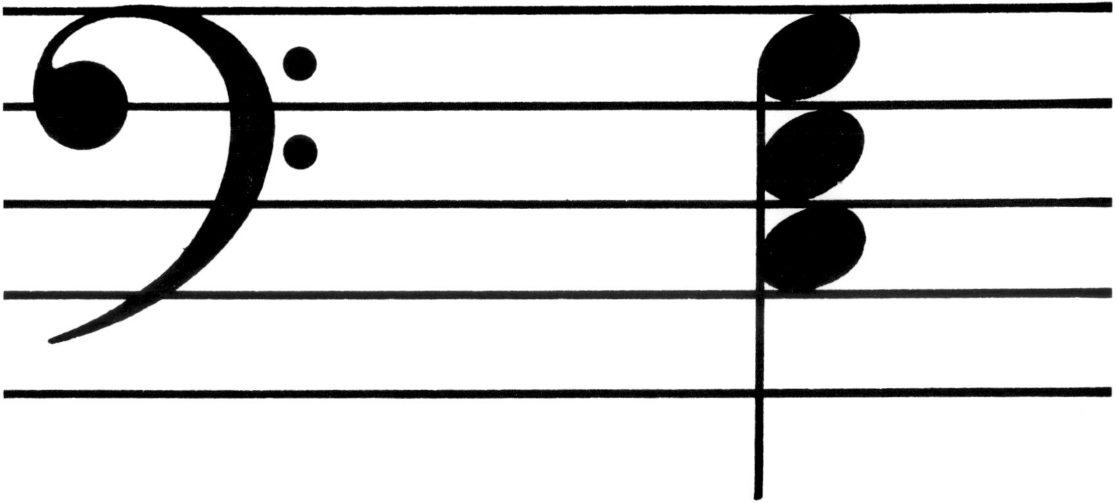

C major

LEE ROBERTS MUSIC PUBLICATIONS, INC.

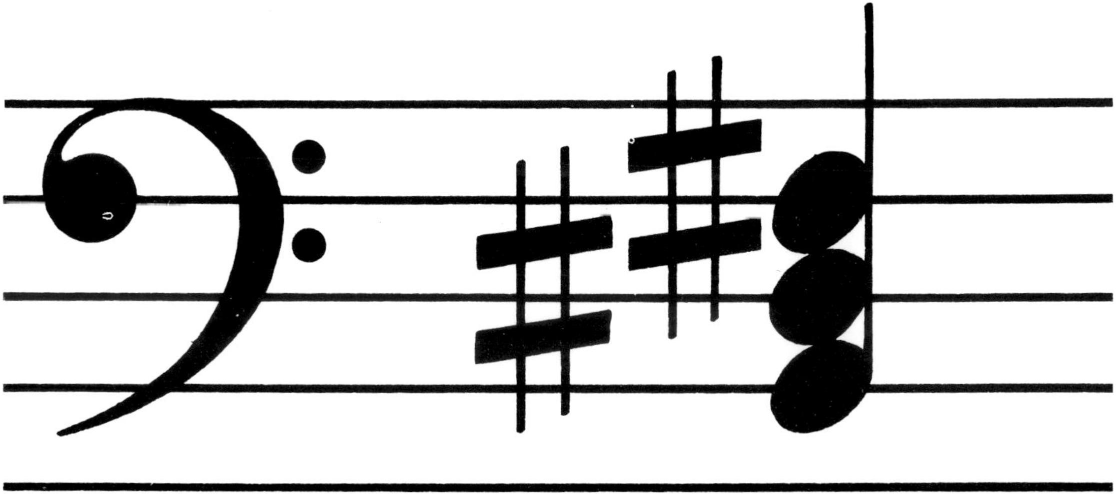

B major

LEE ROBERTS MUSIC PUBLICATIONS, INC.

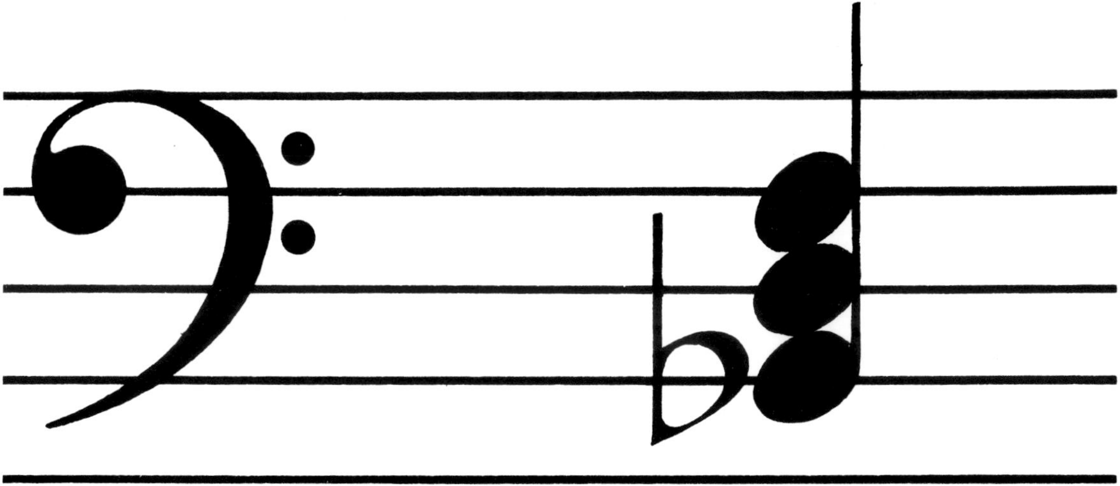

B♭ major

LEE ROBERTS MUSIC PUBLICATIONS, INC.

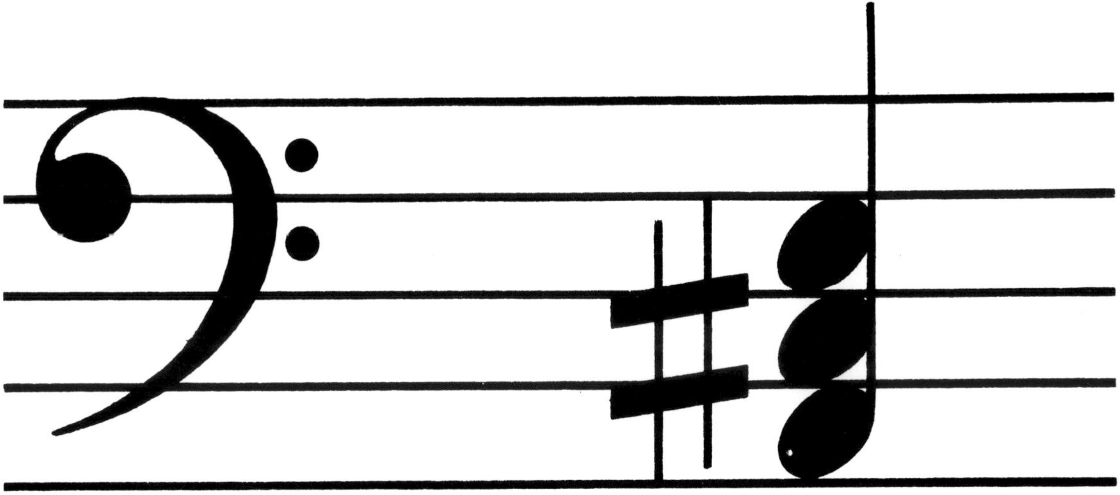

A major

LEE ROBERTS MUSIC PUBLICATIONS, INC.

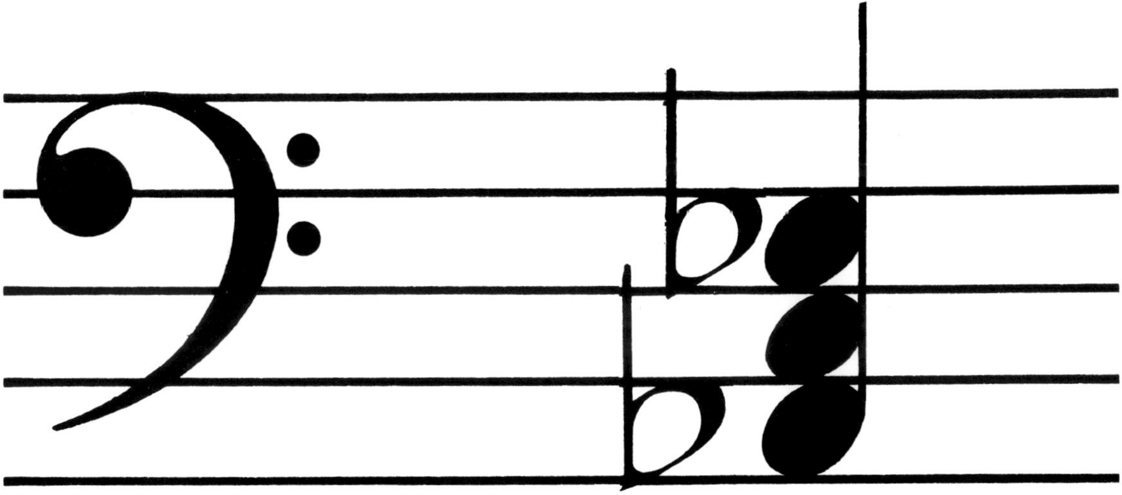

$A^{\flat}$ major

LEE ROBERTS MUSIC PUBLICATIONS, INC.

G major

LEE ROBERTS MUSIC PUBLICATIONS, INC.

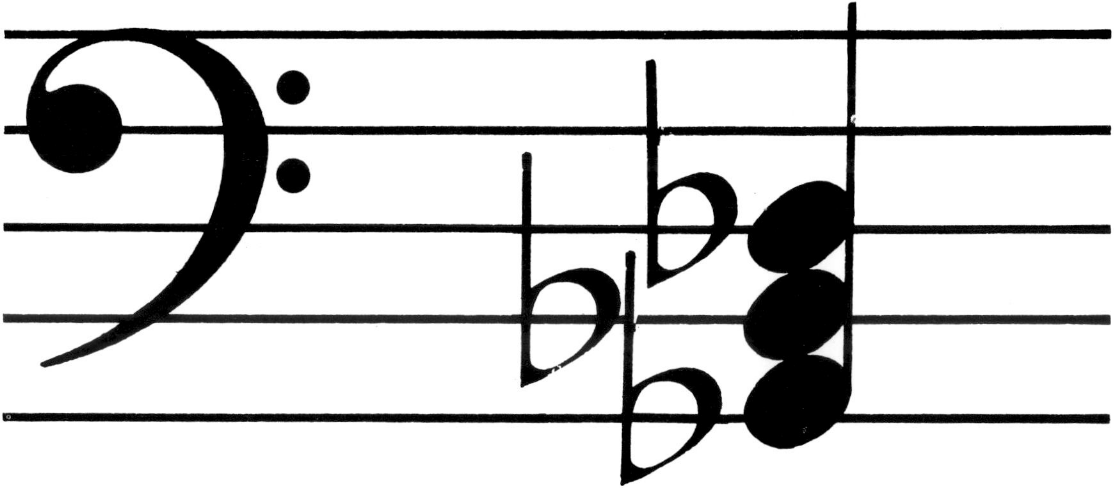

G♭ major

LEE ROBERTS MUSIC PUBLICATIONS, INC.

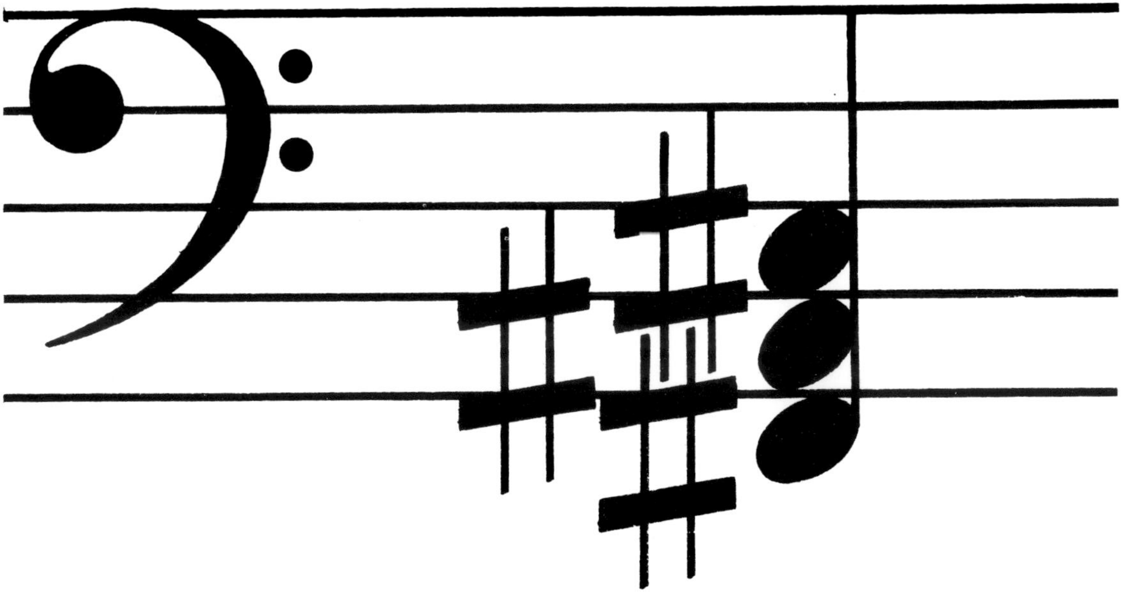

F# major

LEE ROBERTS MUSIC PUBLICATIONS, INC.

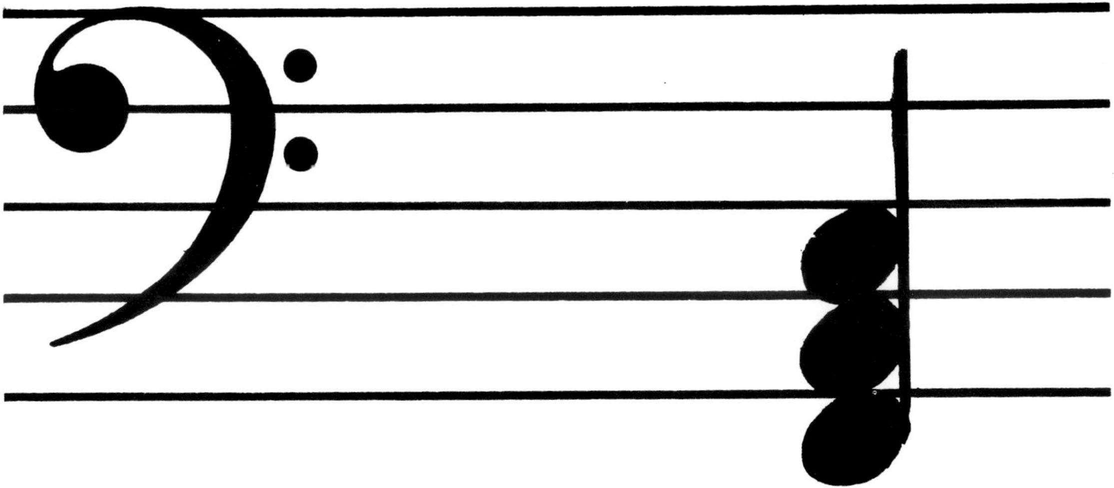

F major

LEE ROBERTS MUSIC PUBLICATIONS, INC.

U.S. $5.95

ISBN 0-634-00178-7

0 73999 72119 5

HL00372119